BIOSPHERES

FROM EARTH TO SPACE

BIOSPHERES

FROM EARTH TO SPACE

Dorion Sagan
and
Lynn Margulis

ENSLOW PUBLISHERS, INC.

Bloy St. & Ramsey Ave.   P.O. Box 38
Box 777   Aldershot
Hillside, N. J. 07205   Hants GU12 6BP
U.S.A.   U.K.

Library of Congress Cataloging-in-Publication Data

Sagan, Dorion, 1959-
    Biospheres from earth to space / by Dorion Sagan and Lynn Margulis.
        p. cm.
    Bibliography: p.
    Includes index.
    Summary: Describes the earth biosphere as a closed ecological system and tells how humans are developing small-scale biospheres to allow them to live in space.
    ISBN 0-89490-188-5
    1. Biosphere—Juvenile literature. 2. Closed ecological systems—Juvenile literature. 3. Closed ecological systems (Space environment)—Juvenile literature. [1. Biosphere. 2. Closed ecological systems.] I. Margulis, Lynn, 1938-   II. Title.
QH313.S25 1989   88-11182
333.95—dc19   CIP
                                                            AC

Printed in the United States of America

10 9 8 7 6 5 4 3 2 1

Illustration Credits:
J. Steven Alexander: pp. 16, 18, 43, 51, 58, 63, 66, 74; Christie Lyons: pp. 59, 64; Sheila Manion-Artz: pp. 16, 25, 67, 74; Laszlo Meszoly: pp. 20, 50; Courtesy of NASA: pp. 56, 57, 86.

To this and future generations, who may be the first
to venture off the Earth and dwell in space.

Acknowledgments

We are most grateful to Wendy Ruther, who helped with the writing and composition of this book from the beginning. Thanks also go to Theresa Chan, Rene Fester, Gail Fleischaker, Carolyn Lupfer, Mary Kay Melvin, Carl Pisaturo, Lorraine Olendzenski, Rae Wallhaussen, and Nat Scholz for work on the manuscript, the index, and the figures.

We thank the artists for their imaginative drawings: J. Steven Alexander, Christie Lyons, Sheila Manion-Artz, and Laszlo Meszoly. The authors received help acquiring information and illustrations from Paul Strother, Umesh Banerjce, William Ormerod, and from those working on Biosphere II in Arizona.

Our sincere appreciation goes to the Lounsbery Foundation and its director, Alan McHenry, for generous and timely financial support. Lounsbery, NASA Life Sciences, and Boston University all participated in funding this work by permitting the employment of several talented students.

Finally, we are grateful to Enslow Publishers for their careful work on the production of this book. Collaborating with our editor Patricia Culleton has been a pleasure.

—D.S.
—L.M.

Contents

1

Living in the Biosphere

Imagine for a moment you are building a large ship that will travel through space. The vessel will be tightly closed and must hold everything you'll need to exist for the rest of your life. For now we're not talking about television and books and musical instruments—objects that impart to your life its special qualities—but just those things that you need in order to live and breathe.

You can probably name most of the things you'll have to put in the spaceship: water, food, and air to breathe. You'll probably need to include some clothes and bedding—and a toothbrush and some soap, too. But even if you could make a list of everything you'd need, it wouldn't be enough—not for very long, anyway. Eventually, you'd run out of food and water unless you could grow or find more.

And what do you think would happen when the air in the ship ran out? Where would you get more? As you keep breathing in and out, the air would get pretty stale; you'd need some way to replenish it and keep from choking.

Where would you get the energy to fuel your daily ac-

11

tivities? How about the temperature—how would you keep it from getting too hot or too cold? How would you get rid of your waste? What would you do when your clothes got dirty? Even if you had a washing machine, where would you get clean water and soap?

These are the kinds of questions you'd have to answer if you were going to live in your ship for a long time on a trip into outer space. It's not enough simply to "camp out" in space. You need to *recycle* your air, water, and food. If you did that, you might live your whole life inside such a ship. So far such ships don't exist. But there are scientists who are trying to answer the very questions we asked above. They are trying to figure out how to keep life going in a closed setting. That way people could live in space indefinitely without the cost of importing supplies.

To create such ships, we must look at the "ship" we're on now. We're all traveling on this planetary ship at over 1000 miles (1600 kilometers) per hour, speeding away from other stars as the Earth spins 24,902 miles (39,843 kilometers) a day. It's as though we're on a very luxurious cruise ship. Luckily, "spaceship Earth" is on automatic pilot. Its controls are unmanned. Not only do we not have to drive it, but it carries with it everything we need.

And if the Earth were a luxury liner, its accommodations for life go beyond any mechanical life-support system. It's almost as if part of the ship were alive. That's right—you, your friends, grass, trees, birds, clouds, and just about everything else at the surface of the Earth are part of a giant living system. We call this system the biosphere.

A biosphere contains everything necessary for life—for you and for all the species of animals and plants and microorganisms that make their homes on the Earth. The biosphere includes nearly everything on the Earth's surface. It spans the seas, lakes, and streams, going down about 6 miles (11 kilometers) into the abyss of the ocean. And it stretches into the atmosphere above us, about 4.6 miles (8 kilometers) high, to the top of the troposphere.

On the Earth just about everything recycles except the pollution from factories and cars—which comes back to haunt us as acid rain and other environmental toxins. Indeed, recycling is the very crux of life, a sort of biological fountain of youth. Recycling keeps nature fresh. Cells, which make up all living things, stay cells by continually taking in some chemicals and putting out others. For example, in seven years most atoms in your body will be different—yet you will be substantially the same person, having many of the same memories. This mysterious turnover of matter also happens to the entire biosphere. The air you breathe, the water in your body and in the oceans, and the complex carbon chemicals that make food and living cells are constantly changing as they move in and out of organisms in a giant circular flow. The substances are reused, and that is why we can think of the biosphere—the planetary system of life—as recycling in a manner similar to a single cell or the human body.

The atmosphere may be thought of as the circulatory system of a giant being. Just as blood flows through our veins and arteries to bring oxygen and nutrients to the cells of muscles, organs, and brain, so winds and rain circulate chemicals around the biosphere. You continually breathe out gases into the atmosphere. Our bodies also produce wastes—feces, urine, and sweat—which become part of the environment. Since these are biodegradable, they are continually being broken down and then put back into the air.

The oceans are also important to the worldwide cycling and storage of chemicals used to make up and break down living beings. The biosphere begins at the ocean floor, about as deep as 6 miles (10 kilometers) beneath the surface. Imagine swimming to the bottom of the sea. You see another world with underwater mountains and submerged peaks. It is dark and cold down here. At 39 degrees Fahrenheit (4 degrees Celsius), the water temperature hovers around freezing. Sunlight doesn't penetrate down this far. The bottom of the sea even has its own lakes: stagnant pockets of warm or cold water that don't mix well with the water of different temperatures around them.

Life probably began at the sunlit surface of the shallow ocean (Fig. 1), but it outgrew its humble beginnings. The biosphere expanded, and now we see organisms living on the bottom of the sea. There goes a deep-sea fish now, its body

Figure 1.

having adapted to the extreme pressures. You can see it because of its "flashlight": glow-in-the-dark bacteria provide it with a natural source of illumination (Fig. 2). Now it swims away, disappearing behind a sunken boulder.

Pressures are extremely high down here. Imagine having over a mile's worth of water pressing in on you from all sides. It's also too dark to permit algae or plants to grow in these depths. Many deep-sea creatures feed instead upon a constant "rain" of tiny bodies and waste falling from above.

If you swim through the darkness, you can feel heat rising from certain cracks on the ocean floor. Here molten rock

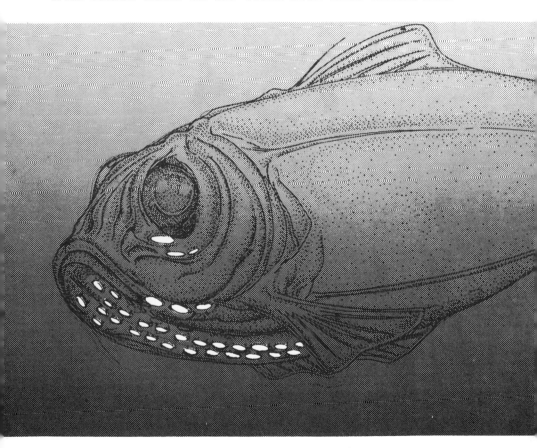

Figure 2.

(lava) bubbles up from inside the Earth. Meeting the icy ocean water, it cools quickly, petrifying into solid pillow-shaped masses. As you pass the pillow lavas on your imaginary swim, you can see what scientists in special submarines have already observed: underwater gardens of unusual life forms. Clams, rare fish, and worms hang around near the hot cracks in the ocean floor; heat coming from the Earth's interior keeps the marine animals warm. Attached to rocks, giant red tube worms almost 5 feet (1.5 meters) tall sway to the deep water currents (Fig. 3). Look—here comes an octopus crawling, tangling up its eight pointy arms.

Figure 3.

16

Sometimes called "octopuses' gardens" but more often known as deep-sea vents, we've only known about these strange places at the bottom of the ocean since 1977. The community of animals here live differently than do organisms on the surface. The red tube worms, for instance, don't eat plants or animals. They don't even have mouths. Instead, they get their food chemically: sulfur bacteria living in special packages grow inside the worms and produce food for themselves and for the worms. Gas bubbling out from the vents with the molten rock enters the blood of the tube worm and from there is carried to the bacteria. The sulfur bacteria take on the gas and act as little food factories in the special packages. That is how the worms "feed." Down here life depends on these cells, able to grow in the total dark by tapping into chemical changes occurring when hot rock simmers up at the floor of the ocean.

Now let's continue our voyage, going from the biosphere's bottom to its top. Imagine swimming up through the ocean, crashing through the surf, and flying into the sky. You are now in the troposphere. This is the part of the Earth's atmosphere where we find weather: wind, rain, clouds, fog, or even smog. Even on the ground we breathe tropospheric air every day (Fig. 4). The higher up into the troposphere we travel, the colder it gets. (You can observe this fact if you sit next to an emergency exit in an airplane.) Above the troposphere, in the part of the atmosphere called the stratosphere, the air starts warming again. But you can never breathe stratospheric air because it is so exceedingly thin, so much like a vacuum, that breathing it would make you feel terribly queasy. And up here you would "pop open." On the surface of the Earth, the pressure inside your body matches that of the surface. Once in the stratosphere, however, your organs would literally burst through your skin. There is not

17

enough pressure to keep you intact. Therefore, you need protection from the lack of pressure if you're going to go into the stratosphere. In space, you need some sort of shell or skin, some way of keeping the pressure found at the Earth's surface. Indeed, there are many things you need this far up. When you leave the troposphere, you leave the biosphere— and nobody can live for long outside of a biosphere.

The Earth's biosphere also includes the rocks and the soil. Soil is rich with assorted life, and so are the puddles and ponds of water that dot the surface of the Earth.

The biosphere, however, is more than all the life that exists within the boundaries just described. It is more like a process, a total recycling system that can be compared to the way the human body operates—constantly changing yet remaining the same. The biosphere also includes the environmental factors that make life possible. The sun energizes the biosphere; the rainfall makes its plants grow. The clouds that

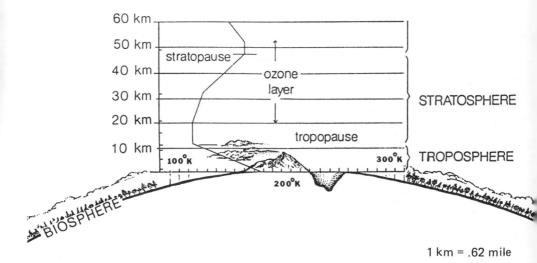

1 km = .62 mile

Figure 4.

18

bring storms, the gases we can't see, garbage and waste—they are all processed and transformed; they are all broken down, winding in and out of each other to form an organization bigger than any organism.

Indeed, the biosphere has the traits of a giant organism. For one thing, though the gases in the atmosphere could react to form stable mixtures, they do not. The same high concentrations of very reactive gases such as oxygen and methane stay in the atmosphere. If you mix reactive gases together they immediately interact, making a chemical reaction. On most planets oxygen and methane would react to form carbon dioxide and water, but on Earth they are continually resupplied to the air. Many very unusual, highly unstable chemicals exist in Earth's air. These include all sorts of organic compounds from the scent of magnolia flowers to butyl mercaptan, the spray of skunks. Our complex atmosphere reflects the diversity of organisms living at the surface (Fig. 5). Lifeless planets do not have such complicated air. Our atmosphere has been built by life; it is as if it were part of a superorganism.

To look at the concept in another way, we know that millions of organisms are being destroyed silently each second, while millions of others are being born. Yet the basic chemical composition of the biosphere does not change. This is similar to your cells growing and dying while you remain pretty much the same.

Another intriguing sign that the biosphere is not that much different from a giant organism comes from astronomy. Many scientists assume the sun used to be smaller and less bright. Yet fossil evidence of life suggests that even the ancient Earth had warm lakes and flowing streams. The temperature at the surface of the Earth was always more or less comfortable, around room temperature. So it seems that as the sun brightened, the Earth cooled itself off. Probably life forms at the surface removed certain "greenhouse" or heat-trapping gases from the atmosphere. Such temperature control—we do it whenever we shiver or sweat, sit in the shade or pick up a fan—is a characteristic of a complex living organism. Computer models show that groups of organisms start controlling themselves like single organisms. Chemicals cycle through the ground, ocean, and air. Like our bones, parts of the seashore store calcium-rich rocks. The concentration of salts in our blood is near that of the oceans, partly because life began in the ocean. The biosphere is so complex that it may be better to think of it as a huge living thing rather than as just a machine.

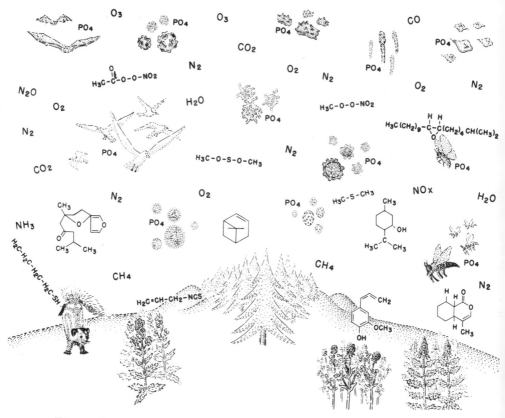

Figure 5.

But if the biosphere can be conceived as a sort of giant organism, it is not like any animal we know. It exhibits far less order, less symmetry. Different places on the Earth have different temperatures and receive different amounts of rainfall and energy from the sun. Though ultimately interwoven, we can break the biosphere up into five major living regions: the coastal zones or seashores, the temperate forests, the deserts, the mountains, and the tropical forests.

Within these five basic major regions are still other smaller regions, or subregions, which can be very different from each other. For example, the seashores in New Jersey and Puerto Rico have great sandy beaches; along other seas are smelly, muddy shores full of microscopic life such as bacteria and tiny burrowing worms (Fig. 6). The marsh smells are usually due to sulfur chemicals produced by microbes that live away from the air in the mud because they are poisoned by

Figure 6.

oxygen. Still other seacoasts, such as those off Maine or Canada's Nova Scotia, are rocky, with great cliffs or small hills of hard rock that extend right down to the water. Every day as the tides come in, rock crevices fill up with water, mixing land and ocean life. As the tides go back out, the crevices drain.

These three kinds of shores—sandy, rocky, and muddy—are only some examples of the kinds of seashores, and the seashores themselves are only one of the major types of regions of the biosphere. Each region and subregion supports different plants, animals, and microorganisms, and each organism or group of organisms may have a role in the functioning of the biosphere. The fish that you find in the water in one subregion of the biosphere—say, the Arctic—are totally different from those you would find in another—say, off a Hawaiian island. They have slightly different lifestyles and feed on different creatures.

Although some living things such as sea grass, earthworms, and houseflies can be found nearly everywhere on the Earth, most organisms stay where conditions are suitable to their special needs and ways of life. One kind of tiny fungus, for example, lives only on the legs of certain spiders. Another species, a kind of tiny moth, lives only in the fur of three-toed sloths dwelling high in the trees of Central and South America. The only time the moths leave the fur is when the sloths descend from the trees once a week to defecate. The female moths lay their eggs on the sloth feces, which provide the larvae with all their minimum daily requirements.

All the organisms found in a particular area at the same time are considered a community. For example, in a forest community on the East Coast of the United States, you would find oak, maple, pine, and birch trees. You would see smaller plants such as grass, clover, asters, and goldenrod. The plants give shelter and energy to woodpeckers, owls, porcupines, skunks, squirrels, raccoons, insects of all kinds, sowbugs, spiders, earthworms, mushrooms, yeasts, bacteria, and many other living beings. If you look at a drop of pond water under a microscope, you can see another whole world of life acting on a smaller scale (Fig. 7).

Due to different conditions such as increased temperature and less rainfall, a sharply different community inhabits the Arizona desert. Here are cacti, mesquite (a prickly shrub that forms pods), kangaroo rats, termites, roadrunners, and many other organisms that can tolerate dryness and hot weather.

Actually, the human body is itself a community of organ-

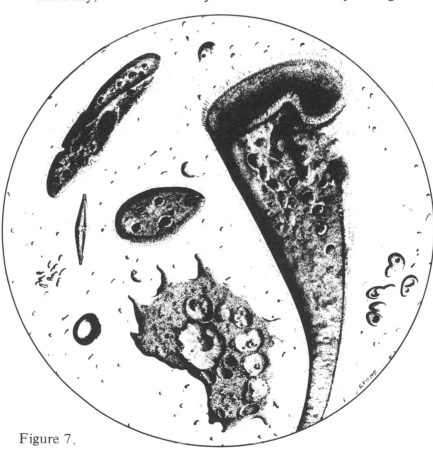

Figure 7.

isms. Imagine for a moment that your cells and tissues were by magic to suddenly disappear. What would be left would be a ghostly film of the bacteria, viruses, fungi, roundworms, and pinworms that normally live on your skin (Fig. 8). Where your stomach and intestines were a moment ago would be part of the ghostly film because they contain intense crowds of yeast and bacteria. These "germs" are normal. In fact, we *need* the microorganisms in our guts to digest food properly. And from a historical point of view, each one of our body's cells may have once been a collection of separate kinds of bacteria. We will have more to say on this subject later. For

Figure 8.

now, it is important to remember that in the same way the biosphere exhibits some of the characteristic traits of a single organism, so the individual is in many ways a collection or aggregate of organisms. These organisms were not originally, nor are they still in many cases, of the same type. They may have even been hostile, invading and eating each other.

The Greeks had a word—*chimaera*—for a mythological creature that was a mixture of various animals, different types of organisms (Fig. 9). A chimera might have the foreparts of a lion, the belly of a goat; or it might be part serpent or have multiple heads. From this animal the adjective "chimerical" has come into our language to describe something unreal or fantastically improbable. Yet in a very real sense we are chimeras: each person represents a community of a great many copies of various types of organisms all acting together as a concerted whole. It is interesting in this connection that

Figure 9.

in English we say "you are" and not "you is." It is as if there were a silent recognition of the fact that each individual embodies not one being but a mass of them, as richly interwoven as a section of the Amazonian forest.

When you take the community of living organisms that inhabits a particular place and add all of the environmental factors that make it unique, you have an ecosystem. Ecosystems are living units, and when you add together all the ecosystems that there are on the planet Earth, you get the biosphere, ranging from a little more than 6 miles (10 kilometers) down into the ocean to a little less than 6 miles (10 kilometers) up into the atmosphere. Though less integrated in its parts than are you, the biosphere is a far greater mix of organisms. It is immensely heavier and more complex, and it has incomparably more organisms working together—both destructively and constructively—in a kind of dynamic harmony.

2

Symbiosis and Homeostasis

The members of a community depend upon one another for survival. In the forest, for example, all the pine, fir, and hemlock trees you see are actually connected directly to the mushrooms growing underneath them. The mushrooms grow from long, thin threads that are intertwined with the tiny root hairs of the trees. These root hairs suck up nutrients such as phosphorus, nitrogen, and sulfur from the mushrooms. In return, the trees feed the mushrooms by sending sugar water through their root hairs. Trees and mushrooms cooperate; they help each other to live. In the same way, mold grows on South American leaf-cutting ants; working together, they can strip the leaves off an orange tree in a single night. The ants employ the mold as a food processor to cut up their food; the mold, growing in great underground gardens deep within ant hills, has its meals collected for it. Completely different species thus help each other; they grow interdependent and ultimately inseparable. Both are big winners.

This type of interdependence between two or more different organisms in a community is known as *symbiosis*. What one organism produces or what changes it makes in the environment may be critical to the survival of another organism. Your body contains many symbionts, such as the bacteria in your mouth and intestine. Your skin is covered by spherical and stringy bacteria that live in its microscopic mountain ridges and valleys. There is even a common microorganism that lives on the surface of the human eye. Certain bacteria in your body make the B and K vitamins you need, whether or not you take vitamin pills. The partnership is between you and your important bacteria living in your intestine, making complex compounds for themselves with enough left over for you. The most successful life forms aid others. We are more aware of threatening organisms, but helpful nondisease organisms are far more common. The vitamin-producing "germs," like others in your gut, float in a virtually inexhaustible stream of what to them is delicious food (Fig. 10).

When you think about symbiosis, think about an orchestra. A community is like an orchestra where each of the musicians has a part to play. Each one listens to the others to know just when to play. What sounds like a whole piece of music is really composed of parts. The music results from many instruments coming together in a single harmonious unity. In fact, our word "organism" comes from the Greek *organon*, meaning instrument. When someone doesn't play his or her part properly, the harmony is disrupted. The conductor or band leader may make a motion to bring whoever it is back into the sonic swing of things. In the same way, if a tree doesn't get enough phosphorus from its mushroom threads, the tree "signals" the mushrooms by not producing enough sugar for the mushroom threads to grow. Mushrooms that give their tree more phosphorus will be rewarded by more food coming back to them. Again we see that successful organisms are not usually fighting but rather flourishing in harmony with their neighbors.

Evolution is not just a bloody battle in which only the vicious survive. Working together is just as important. In fact, as animals go, human beings are relatively powerless, lacking horns, long fangs, fast legs, sharp claws, and so on. But we make up for the lack of such things by using our brains, which allow us to hook up to other organisms, to ride horses, to tame animals, to cultivate plants, and to use wood, rock, and metal from the environment. Organisms working together are stronger than those going it alone. Organisms depend upon

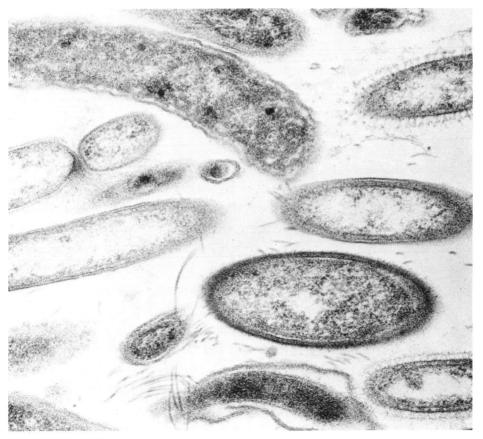

Figure 10.

each other for resources. An ultra-powerful organism that destroys all its neighbors destroys its environment and itself. The best way to kill organisms is to wreck their environment. The deadliest parasites do that for themselves: they kill their host. In so doing, they destroy their own home, and leave themselves out in the cold. Not surprisingly, the deadliest parasites are among the first to die.

Of course, ecosystems do not really need "conductors." Organisms create harmony quite unconsciously by producing one another's foods and consuming one another's wastes. By so doing, they form interconnected systems of new, bigger organisms on a larger scale. Past beings have found that the only way to survive is by compromise, acting in concert. People, too, can no longer afford to grow at the expense of other organisms and the environment at large. To preserve ourselves means preserving the biosphere. We are part of the biosphere.

Individuals, communities, and the planetary living system as a whole actively keep a balance. Symbiosis, and many other relationships between organisms (for example, those between predators and prey, or between pollinators such as bees or bats and the flowers they fertilize) uphold that balance. Homeostasis is the maintaining of balance. Homeostatic systems stay the same despite external changes. If you enter the same oak grove—even after many years—you will find more or less the same number of oak trees. Even though each tree may have made as many as 8,000 seeds during the last year, only one or two, if any, seeds have grown into trees. Those that grow replace the one or two that have died, thus keeping the forest community in balance. And the "lost" seeds have not been wasted but instead have been used as food for fungi, bacteria, worms, and myriads of other organisms.

A nonliving example of homeostasis is a thermostat. Such

30

a device turns on the heating element when the temperature in a room drops; it turns off the heat when the temperature rises. Thus a thermostat constantly reacts to preserve a balance. Similar mechanisms are acting naturally all the time in living beings. For example, when you walk into a cold room, you put on a sweater or start shivering; when you go into the summer sun, you wear loose clothing or start perspiring. By shivering or perspiring, by donning a warm coat or bathing suit, you alter your behavior to keep your temperature the same.

Recycling is also a kind of homeostasis, though instead of maintaining temperature, it maintains form. By continually importing and exporting disposable materials, an adult organism keeps its shape. Homeostasis basically means changing to stay the same. Without it, there would be no biosphere and no life. Chemicals on the surface of the Earth would react with each other to form stable compounds, and the biosphere, instead of maintaining its activity, would become lifeless and dead. The Earth would then be the same as nonliving planets, rather than the same as it was—alive.

3

What's in the Biosphere?

Scientists estimate that the biosphere contains some thirty million species. No census has been taken, but it is clear that there are far more than have been officially identified and described in journals. For instance, if a specialist picks up a handful of soil from a tropical forest, she has a good chance of finding an insect never before discovered by other scientists. Furthermore, over 99 percent of species are extinct, known only from their fossils.

It used to be thought that anything living was either a "plant" or an "animal." But what then is a *Euglena*—a green one-celled creature that thrashes about and swims? Or *Convoluta,* green worms that don't eat but get their nutrition from an internal garden of seaweed? They lie in the sun like algae but crawl into the sand if you walk too close. And bacteria? Can you call them plants or animals when they are neither but evolved into both? To solve such problems, we now have a new system of classification that divides all organisms in the biosphere into five kingdoms (Fig. 11). We have not only plants and animals, but also fungi (such as molds and mushrooms), protoctists (such as paramecia and amebas), and the bacteria. There are at least 500,000 plant, 200,000 protoctist, 100,000 fungal, and 10,000 to 20,000 bacterial species.

Bacteria were the first kingdom to develop and for some two billion years ruled the Earth. In a way, they still do, since more complex cells came from bacteria evolving and living inside one another. The old bacterial biosphere still operates within the present biosphere but has been supplemented. The plant kingdom is important in the new biosphere as a provider of food; animals turn this food into energy and spread nutrients on a global scale by their swimming, burrowing,

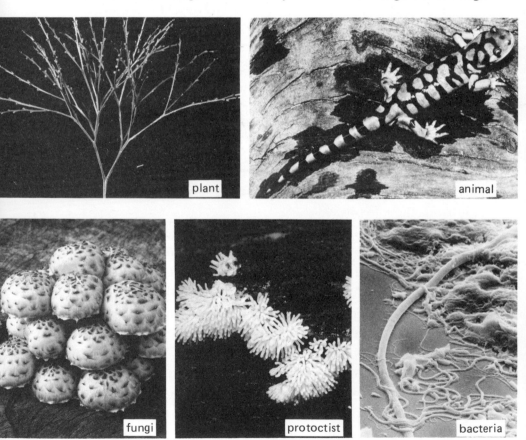

plant

animal

fungi

protoctist

bacteria

Figure 11.

34

sensing, and flying activities. The fungi help spread forests, turn rock into soil, and rot dead bodies back into life-giving nutrients. The protoctist kingdom includes organisms that don't fit neatly into any of the other kingdoms. Like the bacteria, they may be single-celled or multicellular, and their great variety aids in many different biospheric functions.

Each form of life on the Earth depends on the biosphere. Every organism from the most microscopic bacterium to yourself needs a steady supply of elements to maintain and grow. The key elements you need are carbon, oxygen, hydrogen, nitrogen, phosphorus, and sulfur. We are continually making our bodies from these elements combined into various compounds. Proteins, found in all living things, are made of carbon, hydrogen, oxygen, nitrogen, and sulfur, while your genes are made of carbon, hydrogen, oxygen, nitrogen, and phosphorus. Other elements, such as calcium, iron, and potassium, are also used by all forms of life. But they are plentiful on the Earth and used in living bodies in only very small quantities. As vitamins and minerals, these secondary elements are important but not so much as the main bioelements, which are not that abundant in the biosphere and yet are absolutely needed. Without a good supply of nitrogen and phosphorus, for example, growth stops. Organisms starve and die.

It is a mystery that the elements of life are not life but are continually needed by life to re-create itself. For example, an oxygen atom does not become "alive" when you breathe it, any more than it "dies" when you exhale. Yet it is part of you, and you are alive. Elements in the outside environment become bioelements inside organisms. As the biosphere grows, more and more substances become integrated into living structures at a more and more rapid pace. Modern technology incorporates new substances such as plastic and certain metals into the global process of living organization.

Life depends also on other nonliving factors—temperature, water, and light. All organisms thrive only within certain temperature ranges, which they sometimes have difficulty regulating for themselves. They often depend upon an externally controlled temperature, which provides them with the right amount of heat for survival. Water, too, is always essential to life as we know it; even desert animals and plants need water. Most important, however, the biosphere feeds on light. All life at the surface ultimately depends on the energy that comes from the sun's light. Solar energy is the power behind almost all ecosystems. (The deep-sea vents are a rare exception.) It is from the sun that "green life"—sun-loving bacteria, seaweed, algae, and trees—get the energy to make food and give off oxygen during photosynthesis. Without such "green life" (seaweed may be red and brown, too) we could not exist. There would not be enough food or enough oxygen. Indeed, even animals that have never seen sunlight—the tube worms living in the abyss of the ocean, for example—need the sun. In breathing, they depend on it to energize the algae that bubble the oxygen they breathe into the ocean.

There are other nonliving constituents of the biosphere, such as rocks, wind, and weather. Some living things—lichens and edible mussels are two examples—live on rocks. In some cases, they slowly become rocks, and the rocks slowly become them (Fig. 12). Life and its environment are so interconnected that some scientists have conceived of life as a sort of moving mineral. Others have thought of rocks and the atmosphere as the "outside body" of life. Really both ideas are correct. Biological organization is not just an individual but a planetary phenomenon. Life is not just something "in here" but part of the entire biosphere. Many plants need wind to blow away their pollen or their seeds. Fires, hurricanes, and tidal waves all affect global life. An organism can survive only if it can tolerate everything in its environment. If it can, it reproduces, spreading out into new environments.

Such spreading out is a problem for people on the Earth. Our ancestors were so smart that they multiplied from only a few thousand individuals in Africa to stretch over the whole planet, covering a good portion of it first with grazing animals, then with farmlands, cities, and interstate highways. A sort of sick joke is that we have been so successful at changing the Earth to suit our needs that it is now so changed it may no longer suit our needs. Ideas play a role in this. For example, it was once thought that families should have as many children as possible. All plants and animals were for people. Our goal was to dominate nature, to use it "to become fruitful and multiply." Such ideas helped our ancestors live in the biosphere. But at the present rate of population growth, there will be

Figure 12.

some ten billion people by the year 2000 A.D. The relationships among living organisms are changing. You can have too much of a good thing, and so can the biosphere.

Ecologists talk about the "carrying capacity" of an environment. This is the quantity of organisms a given environment can support. Carrying capacity varies according to the type of organism—large animals like people need much more room than smaller animals like snails. For example, it takes many square miles to support an elephant but only one square inch to support a nematode worm. The biosphere may have reached its level of support of human growth—the carrying capacity of the earth is being strained, and the environment is suffering. This is especially true since our growth has often been at the expense of other organisms that play a role in maintaining the global environment.

Of course, one way or another, people will come into harmony with the environment. Wars and plagues, birth control, and even adolescent gang fights, suicides, and drug abuse lead to fewer people. From a biological point of view, we don't know exactly how these population controls work. But they seem to be homeostatic mechanisms regulating population growth. Limiting runaway human growth may help reestablish biospheric harmony. We must remember that we are just one tiny part of a huge interconnected living system.

Most people consider humans the most important and advanced species. But the biosphere is far more than people. Like a symphony orchestra, it would not do to have only drummers or cello players. And even if the conductor is the most important part, it certainly would not do to have only conductors! The biosphere is a superorganism. When one part of an organism grows wildly at the expense of its neighboring parts and organs, we say the creature is abnormal or has a disease. Some have compared the spread of technology to a cancer or tumor, but that is not really fair. Pregnancy is also like an illness in that a woman experiences "abnormal" growth. But is it therefore a disease? In the same way, the spread of people and machines represents the biosphere struggling to grow. The biosphere's sickness may end not so much in death as in birth.

Similar events happen to all species. Life is continual striving. Under changing conditions, we have to change simply to survive. Our ideas about the environment affect how we treat the environment. That affects what the environment becomes. We are not the only thinking species, but we are the only one whose thoughts are so easily converted into environmental change. Now more than ever it is important to realize that what we think translates into the way things are. We evolved from the biosphere, and now the biosphere is being transformed to a large extent by our ideas about it.

4

The Changing Biosphere

To understand the changes taking place, think again of the biosphere as if it were a single giant living organism. Each part affects every other. Some parts dramatically impact upon others (the trees and clouds, for example) while others have little global impact. Not only tropical forests, such as are found in the Amazon basin, but also marshlands and muddy seaside expanses that look relatively unimportant may, in fact, be very important parts in the biosphere. Though the biosphere is a whole, parts of it are always moving, growing, feeding, excreting, being born, and dying. When plants use light during photosynthesis and give off oxygen, oxygen enters the atmosphere. When people take in oxygen as they exercise, oxygen comes out of the air. When a beaver gnaws a tree and makes a dam, he provides a pool for algae to grow. These algae make the oxygen that enters the beaver's branched home, and the beaver's offspring breathe clean air at night. This example is only the tiniest indication of the intense interaction among living organisms going on at all times in all parts of the biosphere.

The biosphere must change to exist, but if it were to change too much, life could no longer survive. Remember— there are very specific requirements for life. All organisms must live within a certain temperature range, not too hot and not too cold. Each needs specific things. If there is too much of one thing or not enough of another, or if the temperature is too hot or too cold, organisms die. But their death helps reestablish a dynamic balance by making room for other organisms that can survive. The whole arrangement favors the growth of interconnected groups of organisms that can maintain their environment.

The story of the biosphere—and the fact that there is life on the Earth—is the story of the connections between living organisms and between them and the nonliving factors of the environment. Humans and fungi could not exist without plants; red tube worms on the ocean floor could not exist without a steady supply of sulfur from inside the Earth; woodpeckers could not exist without hollow trees and insects; and nothing could live without a constant supply of water and the steady stream of light from the sun (Fig. 13).

The Earth's ancient system of interacting life in this context has been called "Biosphere I." Biosphere I is the first biosphere, the parent of us all. Scientists study the relationships, connections, and the resulting homeostasis of Biosphere I. One of their goals is to construct new biospheres that can support humans together with other life forms—just as the surface of the Earth does. Creating new biospheres would be a great technological triumph. It might make it possible for people to survive long voyages to other planets, or even to nearby stars. But more important, the creation of biospheres provides a living lesson for the rest of us here in Biosphere I as citizens of an increasingly crowded Earth. Successfully running a new

Figure 13.

biosphere would show people what it takes to make it in our beloved old one. It might teach us how to avoid the pitfalls of pollution and live with our technology in a new harmony with the environment. Once Europeans traveled to the New World. Now scientists, engineers, and architects are working on making new worlds—living copies of "Mother Earth"—our first biosphere.

5

Recycling

As we mentioned, a crucial part of homeostasis is recycling. Remember that the biosphere is closed; nothing much new ever comes from outer space. Solar radiation is the exception; its energy powers the whole recycling planetary system. The elements in the biosphere cycle again and again in global processes of replenishment, regeneration, and rejuvenation. At the same time, the biosphere grows. The production of man-made biospheres is, in a sense, an extension of this ancient process of circulation. We might whimsically call it "rebirth of the Earth."

But let's take a closer look at recycling. Start with your trash and garbage, for example. Where does it go? In some cities, garbage collected in trucks is put into special large "sterilizer trucks," which act as giant pressure cookers. After heat and pressure treatment to get rid of the bacteria and fungi, sanitation workers dump the sterile garbage into pig-feeding bins. The pigs gorge themselves on the remains before bacteria and fungi spoil their food. The pigs grow for a few months, and then they are slaughtered and made into pork products for people so that we can generate more garbage!

Trash (paper, cans, bottles, etc.), by contrast, is usually burned and the remaining ashes used for landfill. Healthy trees and other plants then use the nutrients from the ash to grow. We cut down the trees for paper, or we build houses on the landfill and start gardens—with food plants—in our yards. And so the recycling process goes on and on—for humans and for all other life on Earth.

The recycling process of the body is different because we do not directly recycle our wastes, but we do continually replace our parts on a cell level. The biosphere also does not always completely recycle all its parts but sometimes stores wastes. Sometimes these wastes—such as the coal and oil used by our technological society—find their way back into the global circulation. Coal, for instance, represents the crushed and buried parts of primeval trees (Fig. 14). For mil-

Figure 14.

lions of years the foodlike energy contained in the carbon compounds piled up as an unprocessed waste product. But with the Industrial Revolution, the energy locked up in the coal was released when the coal was burned, sometimes to run machines that extracted more coal from the ground.

Other kinds of mineral deposits are also due to the activities of living organisms. The limestone rocks in Fig. 15 were made by blue-greens living on top of each other and climbing out of their protective sheaths to get at the light. If you look at chalk under the microscope, you will see tiny shells of microorganisms. Even iron and gold deposits may have been

Figure 15.

47

accumulated by iron bacteria and other microorganisms. *Eoastrion,* in a two-billion-year-old rock, is probably a fossil iron bacterium (Fig. 16).

The elements of your body must recycle for you to remain the same, let alone grow. In the same way, global recycling ultimately leads beyond planetary maintenance to planetary growth. "Artificial" biospheres repeat processes of growth that have occurred many times before in evolution, but never on such a large scale. The biospheres are really not artificial but a natural by-product of the ancient process of reproduction.

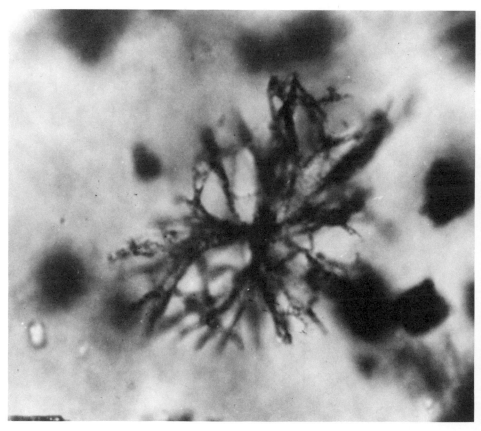

Figure 16.

6

A Day in the Life of
the Biosphere

We know that Biosphere I has changed over the millions of years it has existed because scientists have examined ancient rocks. They looked at the fossils of organisms that were trapped in the rocks and have reconstructed some of the epic story of life's development on the Earth, the growth of the biosphere. One simple way of reconstructing the puzzle of life's history is from bones, as shown in Fig. 17. But there are more subtle ways to know what went on, including an examination of the chemistry of ancient rocks and of life forms that still exist today but are very similar to others preserved in the rock record.

Such methods reveal the following picture. When the Earth was first formed, about four and a half billion years ago, the early atmosphere had little or no oxygen. Then, about two billion years ago, bacteria called blue-greens put so much oxygen into the atmosphere that they changed it forever (Fig. 18). You may see their descendants growing today along shower stalls, in puddles, and on outdoor fountains. The large amount of oxygen in the air spelled widespread death at first.

Figure 17.

Most organisms were not used to the gas in their environment. It acted as a poison, killing them. In fact, the first to be destroyed by the pollution were the blue-greens that produced the oxygen. Eventually, however, organisms adapted to it, but it was primarily up to the polluting species to clean up its act, to adjust to the new wastes its members had created. Humanity today finds itself in a similar position: we also are often the first to have to deal with the effects of our pollution.

The blue-green bacteria were among the first life forms. They originated over three and a half billion years ago. (Their sulfur-using ancestors were photosynthetic but did not give off oxygen.) Instead of water (H_2O), these ancient bacteria used hydrogen sulfide (H_2S) for their source of hydrogen. As waste, they gave off yellow microscopic pellets—sulfur globules. Then mutants arose that developed the knack of using water instead of hydrogen sulfide for their hydrogen.

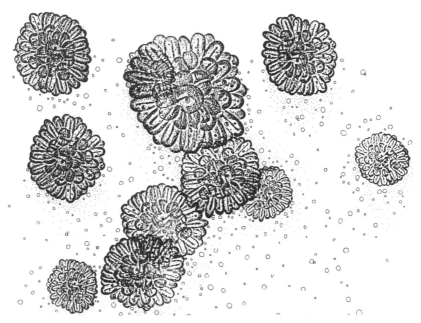

Figure 18.

The mutants were the first blue-greens, and because they used a different food, they produced a different waste—oxygen. Sulfide comes from volcanoes, but water is everywhere. Using water, the blue-greens grew with wild abandon, expanding over wet rocks, standing pools, muddy flats, and damp soil. In light they grew by combining carbon from carbon dioxide with hydrogen from water. As they piled up on the surface of the Earth, carbon dioxide started draining out of the air in huge amounts.

At the same time, the oxygen that was given off by the blue-greens reacted with iron to make rust and with uranium to make uranium oxide. These reactions at first prevented too much of an accumulation of oxygen, but eventually oxygen ran out of minerals to react with and jeopardized life. Oxygen is a very strong gas; it blazes. When people in hospitals or space vehicles use it, they have to be very careful. The oxygen that was added to the biosphere could have killed almost all the early living organisms—because at first there were none capable of living with it. Some organisms swam into the mud; even today oxygen kills them. They stayed away from oxygen forever, just as we today avoid breathing the methane or hydrogen sulfide that they like. Other bacteria, however, survived because they developed a method of using the hazardous oxygen waste. The method, called *respiration,* is the process by which organisms use oxygen to get energy from food in a sort of "controlled burning."

Bacteria evolved that exploited oxygen's fire-feeding nature to quicken their own actions. You developed in part from such bacteria. A microscopic investigation of almost any cell in your body shows it to contain tiny oxygen-using bodies. Called mitochondria, these bodies came from bacteria trapped in animal cells. To this day they even have their own DNA and a bacterial way of reproducing. Scientists believe the ancestors of mitochondria proliferated on an oxygen-polluted Earth. For most, oxygen was a poison, but these organisms turned it from a dangerous irritant into an invaluable fuel.

Humans—and all animals—respire; we all have descended in part from this ancient oxygen-using line of bacteria. When the biosphere was still dominated by bacteria, the oxygen users seem to have been either parasitized or swallowed by other bacteria. The two kinds of organisms adapted to each other and survived. Cooperating, they formed a new, larger kind of cell. These new cells were the forerunners of amebas, paramecia, bread mold, rosebushes, toadstools, African elephants, people, and all other organisms with mitochondria in their cells. The ability to treat toxic fumes as fresh air was so important that cells that couldn't do it teamed up with those that could. Science truth is stranger than science fiction: we are descended from symbiotic aggregates—millions of microbes all working together to form a single body with a unified form and sense of self.

The build-up of oxygen in the atmosphere is one of the best examples we have of life dramatically altering its own environment. Life does not simply adapt to a dead environment. The environment is made up of life and is really alive. The story of the oxygen crisis shows that life often adapts to itself, creating and solving its own problems—and creating new ones. The use of water, for example, solved the problem of dwindling reserves of hydrogen and led to planetary poisoning. So, too, the rise of new cells able to survive the oxygen reinforced the change to a much more dangerous global environment. Our oxygen-rich or *aerobic* atmosphere feeds reactions from forest fires to gunpowder explosions to the burning of gasoline, coal, and oil. It provides our cells with more energy than was ever possible in the old oxygenless atmosphere. But it also leads to new crises of pollution, destruction, and extinction.

7

Biospheres on
Other Planets

Existing in a biosphere that supports life on the Earth, we might think there are biospheres on other planets in the solar system, too. After all, the neighboring planets also get energy from the sun. We'd especially expect to find life in a biosphere on the planets closest to us and most like ours: Mars and Venus. These two planets are just a little smaller than the Earth. Venus (Fig. 19) is a little nearer to the sun than we are, and Mars is a little farther away.

But there are no lakes, rivers, or oceans on Mars or Venus, and there can be no life as we know it without liquid water. Another reason for life not existing on our planetary neighbors is sometimes put in terms of the story of Goldilocks and the Three Bears. Venus is too hot; the tiny amount of water on it is present as steam. Mars is too cold, and the ice remains frozen. Earth is "just right." Yet this conception comes from the old view of life adapting to a static environment. We know now that life has changed the Earth as much as it has adapted to it.

Both Mars and Venus have mostly carbon dioxide in their

atmospheres. The Earth at one time had more carbon dioxide in the air, but the blue-greens, algae, and, later, plants took it out as they grew. The carbon dioxide in the Earth's atmosphere was also transformed by microscopic life into limestone. Now there is less than one percent carbon dioxide in our air; the atmospheres of Venus and Mars, by contrast, consist of over 95 percent of this gas.

In part because of the temperature and the atmosphere of Mars and Venus, organisms never developed there or, if they did, they didn't evolve ways of using carbon dioxide from the air and giving off oxygen. It is only in the biosphere of the

Figure 19.

Earth that we find oxygen gas—and we know that it comes as a waste product of living organisms. All living things take up some gases from the atmosphere and give off others. As a result of these numerous gas exchanges, the Earth's atmosphere has become increasingly different from that of the neighboring planets over three billion years. Our atmosphere has methane and hydrogen gas made by some bacteria, and the soil harbors organisms that use such gases. The atmosphere of the Earth contains lots of complex chemicals in it such as camphor and ragweed pollen (see Fig. 5). The only signs of life on either Mars or Venus—like the Viking lander crouched upon the rusty desert of the red planet—come from the Earth (Fig. 20).

The life that existed on the Earth changed the early atmosphere, and new life forms developed. Today, life continues to affect the characteristics of the Earth's surface. The waste

Figure 20.

from one kind of organism is the food for another kind. Bird guano piles up as white sea islands and mountains. The mountains are mined for phosphorus and nitrogen, which are then used as fertilizer for crops such as rice or corn (Fig. 21).

At the present time, we do not think any other biospheres exist in our solar system. Someday we may discover them in distant solar systems, on planets, or in interstellar space. We may even find ways to detect biospheres in other galaxies. For example, it might already be possible for extraterrestrial scientists to detect life here by a long-distance examination of the gases of our atmosphere. Such an investigation would reveal the simultaneous presence of reactive gases in our atmosphere. Under normal laboratory conditions these gases are expected to react with each other and form more stable mixtures. The reason they coexist in the Earth's biosphere is because they are continually replenished by the recycling activities of life.

Figure 21.

Without any clear sign of alien biospheres, we must for now study the one in which we live. If humans create new life-supporting biospheres, we will not really be studying anything alien but simply grafting or cloning our original biosphere— what the ancient Greeks called *Gaia,* the earth goddess (which provides the English roots for "geology" and "geography"). So-called terraforming—setting up new biospheres on other planets—will come through understanding the way our old one works, with all of its changes, connections, and various forms of life (Fig. 22).

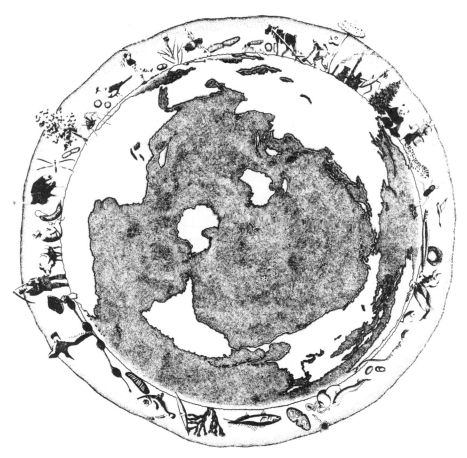

Figure 22

8

Propagules

We think of technology as a strictly human conception, but really it belongs to all life. We can observe this fact quite clearly in biosphere creation. We depend on other organisms to live; thus our self-propagation necessarily will involve the increase of many other forms of life. There is no way, for example, to exclude microbes from a biosphere built for humans. It is almost as if nature is achieving her own ancient ends by playing to our ego, our sense of accomplishment and pride. We must realize that civilization is a phase in the development of the biosphere. It is not the first or the last but part of an ongoing metamorphosis that includes and yet is more than our wildest dreams.

In helping astronauts and cosmonauts get to other planets, scientists are finding that they have to bring many other organisms as part of a life-support network. The technological production of living miniatures of the Earth is admittedly very new, but at the same time it hooks into an ancient process of cooperation, of living parts coming together to form new reproducing wholes.

In the process of reproduction, life defies arithmetic: one equals two. A yeast cell (a kind of fungus) reproduces by budding to form two cells (Fig. 23). A pair of dogs of course reproduce by having puppies. A bread mold reproduces by releasing spores into the air. There are many ways to reproduce; all lead to increasing numbers of organisms (Fig. 24). One organism reproduces to become two, two four. At least some organisms in all five kingdoms reproduce without sex—that is, they have only one parent. In some cases, like that of human beings, two organisms become three in the course of reproduction. But in all cases the number of organisms grows.

Often, however, an organism can't reproduce because the conditions aren't favorable. It may be too cold or too dry; there might not be enough light, food, or breathable air. All sorts of difficulties can keep organisms from growing and reproducing. When this is the case, many organisms have devised a special ploy of making "propagules."

A propagule is a tiny package that some organisms make so that they can survive periods of dryness and lack of food. A propagule is a sort of pod with everything the organism will need to regenerate when conditions change for the better.

Seeds are an example of propagules. Some can remain dormant for years in dangerous environments. Many bacteria make propagules called spores outside their cells. Such bacteria die, but the spores are all that is needed for future growth.

Whatever else an organism includes inside a propagule, there are always genes—the genetic material needed to organize a complete small organism from the surrounding environment. Sometimes a complete immature organism is inside the propagule. Corn kernels, which contain embryos, are an example. Propagules also have in them a ration of food, an initial source of carbon and energy. A little water is also nec-

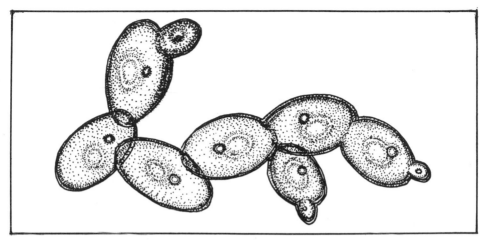

Figure 23.

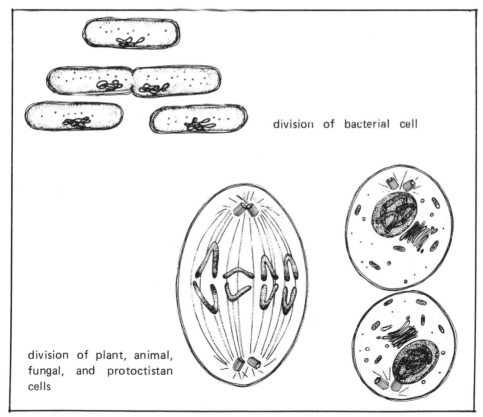

division of bacterial cell

division of plant, animal, fungal, and protoctistan cells

Figure 24.

essary and can be found in even the driest propagules. In summary, propagules represent a sort of closed-off "resting" stage in the life cycles of many organisms.

Propagules also have a delivery method. Bacterial spores or dandelion seeds spread by wind. People propagate corn kernels, which are cloaked in a husk so thick they must be stripped by human hands or technology. Water bears or tardigrades (Fig. 25) change into barrel-shaped forms called "tuns" and can last in this way up to a hundred years. Many kinds of fungus propagules have many small hooks to attach to rat or mouse fur. Such propagules move by animal muscles to new areas, where living space, food, water, and other resources are presumably more plentiful. Other propagules such as fungal spores and tomato seeds have to be swallowed, tra-

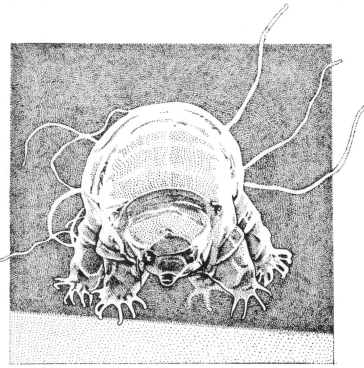

Figure 25.

verse an animal's intestine, and be defecated before they can start to grow again.

Not all species make propagules, but we can find examples of them in each of five kingdoms. In the drawing of members of the five kingdoms (Fig. 26), the *Hydra,* a pond water animal that combines both male and female characteristics, has two conical spermaries on top of it. The spermaries release sperm to fertilize the egg in the nearby ovary, seen as the large bump on the side. After fertilization, a hard egg is made, which slides down the *Hydra* and "sits tight" all winter. In this case the egg—capable of hatching the following spring—is the resistant propagule.

The propagules of the ciliate appear as "bumps" on its rounded surface. As the soil dries out, the propagules will be let loose. Moving with the wind, they will land everywhere. If they happen to light on wet rich dark soil, they will start to grow into little ciliates.

The bacterium looks a bit like a strange microscopic tree forming clusters of "melons." These structures are really propagules. The organism that produces them is a bacterium called *Stigmatella.* The propagules are called myxocysts. If they land on good soil, their hard walls crack open, releasing rod-shaped bacteria fully capable of growth.

The plant, too—a moss called *Polytrichum* or "hairy cap"—makes a brown powder, which upon closer inspection is seen to consist of propagules. They grow into long white threads that eventually turn green and grow if given light and water.

On the underside of the fungus *Amanita* are mushroom gills, along which are propagules called basidiospores. If they can hold out until water again becomes available, they will grow into the threads that eventually form the mushroom body.

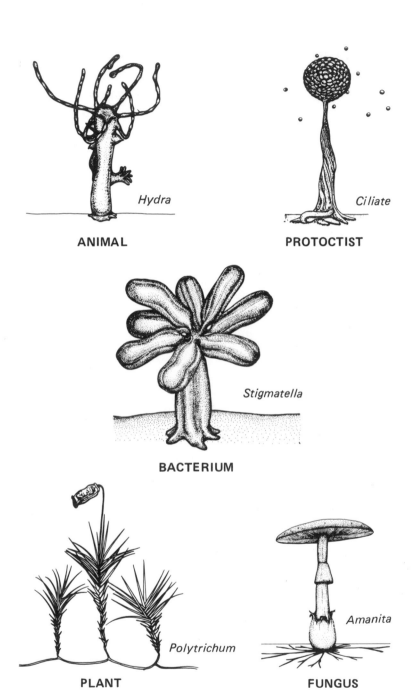

Hydra

ANIMAL

Ciliate

PROTOCTIST

Stigmatella

BACTERIUM

Polytrichum

PLANT

Amanita

FUNGUS

Figure 26.

66

Three kinds of very different propagules are displayed in Fig. 27: bacterial spores, dinomastigote cysts, and walnuts.

Propagules then are marked by three things: (1) the formation of a resistant, protective covering; (2) an absence of active growth; and (3) movement—they have a means of transport or delivery. By these criteria the enclosed ecosystems or biospheres made by human beings are not quite propagules. But if we can transmit life-support systems to space stations or other planets by rocketry or other suitable technology, such an accomplishment would represent the formation of true biospheric propagules—a sort of "seeding" of the entire Earth!

Propagules have arisen many times in evolution. In each species, they represent a similar solution to a common problem. The problems of survival may become overwhelming. Reproduction may occur too quickly. There may be too many organisms of a particular species in one place; the tendency for overcrowding is very common among living organisms. Because they eat the same foods, use the same resources, and pursue the same mates, organisms of the same species often compete more with each other than they do with members of other species. The more successful they are at growing, the

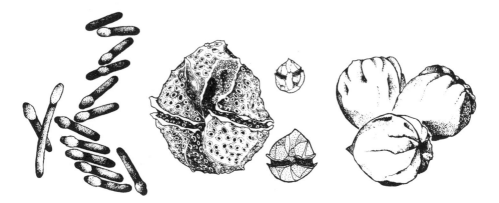

Figure 27.

more likely they are to pollute their local surroundings. Such competition may heighten stress in individuals as they grow in one another's company in a given environment. Ultimately, the only survivors may be those who make propagules or similar protective structures. Such biological packaging prepares organisms to "pack up and leave." Thus streamlined, they can "travel light"—migrate to and settle in more attractive surroundings.

Organisms have been making and refining propagules for millions of years. The most successful ones enable species to survive periods of drought and famine. The earliest propagules were probably bacterial spores such as those of *Clostridia* (Fig. 28). The bacteria themselves grow easily in the absence of oxygen as long as water and food are present. As conditions make growth more difficult, they either die or make resistant spores inside their cells. (They differ in this

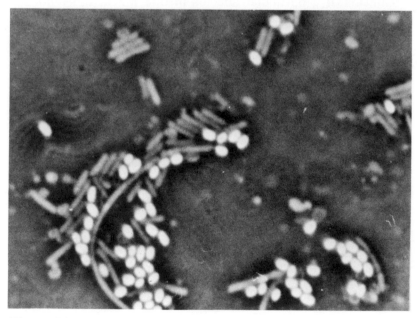

Figure 28.

way from most spore-forming bacteria.) The propagules float through the air and may land anywhere—in your glass, under a contact lens, on the countertop. With enough food and moisture, the propagule "blooms," converting from a restive to an actively growing form.

Historically, humans have not made true propagules. Neither did the great apelike creatures from whom it is thought we evolved. Instead, when times got tough, we have died or sought better environments by traveling across land and ocean. We have become organized into complex societies that provide us with food, water, and protection against cold, wind, and enemies. We have found ways to make life possible in extremely difficult environments, first perhaps by donning animal skins and living in caves and huts. Later we mastered transport and encapsulation technology in such forms as submarines, skyscrapers, and supersonic airplanes. We have developed ship and shelter technologies that supply us with our needs even in extremely hazardous environments. Our food is prevented from spoiling by canning and refrigeration, and there are even sperm banks for humans. All these developments represent a movement toward propagule formation for the human species. But this propagule formation is not at the microscopic level but at the whole Earth scale.

The time is coming when the human species—and through us life itself—will require propagules. For one thing, many of the environments in which we have lived can no longer support healthy life. Too many people in a single place deplete the store of clean water and food. Increasing levels of pollution have begun to deplete the fresh air we need to breathe. If other organisms, such as ciliates and bacteria, have made propagules for millions of years, why can't we? For others, including brine shrimp with their salt-resistant eggs, and dinomastigotes with their "resting cysts" (see Fig. 27), propagules are a natural part of the life cycle. For us so far they have not been; we have always lived and survived by growing as fast as possible without stopping or looking backward. But it seems as if we should now be looking backward to the successful strategies used by life in the past.

A time is coming when countries may build enclosed propagules simply to ensure clean air, unpolluted water, and pesticide-free food for their citizens. It is not hard to imagine such structures popping up all over the surface of the Earth. It would be similar to increased private property ownership when people found they had to own land or risk its being ruined by others. Some have even suggested that human-built biospheres might provide protection in case of nuclear war; this premise, however, seems extremely doubtful. Biospheres being built now admit light: they are literally "glass houses," and the darkening of the world from dust and soot following fires in cities and war zones would halt plant life in these biospheres as well as anywhere else.

It might be better of course if we stopped our own rampant growth. Pollution and related stresses due to an overabundance of our own kind would subside. Biospheres could even provide a lesson to help us curb global population growth. By dramatically focusing on a total living system, people would see that life needs many forms working in harmony, and they might be induced to pay more attention to restoring their natural environment. We might be less furiously driven by the profit motive. If everybody does only what is good for his or her own pocketbook, it is going to hurt all of us. Whereas if we consider the welfare of others, now and in the future, we will stop short of trying to make a buck when it threatens the common environment. Public attention to the fact that we all inhabit one Earth might then prevent global pollution and a new era of "haves" and "have-nots"—those with and without access to purifying biospheres.

There is a place in the future for automobiles, technology, and vast human civilizations. However, to preserve ourselves, we must preserve the natural environment of which we are a part. Biosphere I can do without us—it did for eons before we evolved—but we cannot do without it.

Another reason we may need to create propagules is because the environment of outer space is far more hostile than any here on Earth. If we want to travel to, and perhaps live in, outer space beyond the biosphere, we will have to create a special kind of propagule. Only a very complex re-creation of life on Earth can insure the mental health of biosphere inhabitants.

What will we need in our propagule? How small can a biosphere be? What sorts of life forms do we need? Wouldn't we get claustrophobic? If closed up entirely to everything but light, can a community of organisms survive? For how long?

We aren't the only ones asking these questions. At this very moment people in various countries are working to create enclaves in which life, including human life, becomes self-sustaining. People have been thinking about the problem for decades, but serious efforts are now under way in the Soviet Union, Japan, the United States, and other countries. As we suggested earlier, developing such technology is crucial for getting life into space, as well as for improving our knowledge of life on Earth. The race to conquer inner space by building biospheres may prove even more exciting than the race to put a person on the moon.

9

Ecospheres

Ecospheres are desk-top living universes. The organisms inside the glass spheres form a closed system with everything they require to keep going. They are unlike other aquariums in that they never need to have food added or their water changed. No outside maintenance is required. Just put one on your windowsill, and it will recycle with internal harmony and last for years.

Inside a crystal orb swim from six to ten tiny Hawaiian fairy shrimp. Ranging from clear to pink or orange, the shrimp constantly flutter, nibbling at the green algae growing with them (Fig. 29). They can be seen reflected in the glass, magnified as they navigate the contours of their miniature ocean.

As in our world, which is 24,902 miles (39,843 kilometers) rather than several inches in circumference, the ecosphere organisms cooperate; they exist in mutual dependence. Carefully selected by scientists rather than evolved over immense stretches of time, the organisms achieve an internal harmony. The algae grow by using carbon dioxide breathed out by the

73

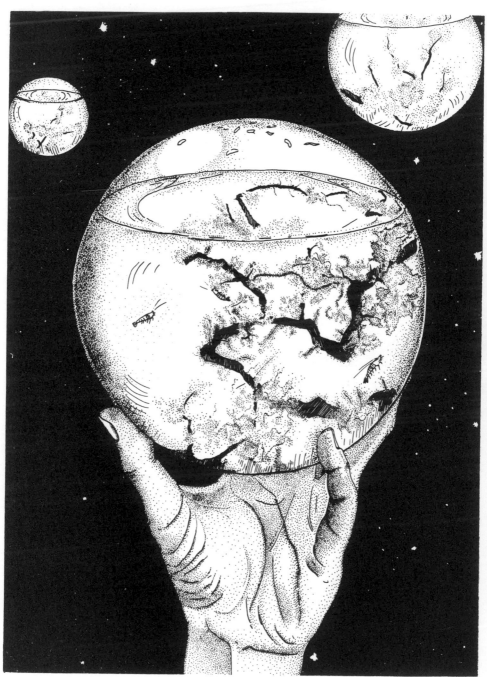

Figure 29.

fairy shrimp. Shrimp waste fertilizes them. For their part, the shrimp breathe the oxygen produced as waste by the underwater forests. Many protists and bacteria invisible to the naked eye are also involved in the self-perpetuating cycles of the ecospheres. And, as in our biosphere, sunlight is the ultimate energy source, powering the entire system. (Extraterrestrial life forms running ultimately on light may have advanced far beyond their one-planet homes. They may grow in huge circles around stars, making use of the light. Physicist Freeman Dyson has suggested that we might search distant suns for signs of such huge disks or spheres.)

Some of the ecospheres have been alive and well for over a decade. The eyes of some owners lit up when they noticed their shrimp had reproduced! No one knows exactly what the proportion is of various kinds of bacteria and other microorganisms inside an ecosphere. No one knows either if there is some absolute upper limit on how long such a small system can last. Most ecospheres, if they are kept within a comfortable temperature range so that they don't become an ice ball or shrimp bisque, last for about three years. But ecospheres aren't biospheres; they are not propagules but a step toward propagules. They are not resistant to extreme conditions, and they don't start growing again. Most fairy shrimp captured in ecospheres don't reproduce. Yet at the same time ecospheres show that organisms *can* live for extended periods in isolation. And not just any organisms but *animals,* oxygen-breathing organisms not unlike ourselves.

10
Biosphere II

Those making ecospheres are not the only ones working on propagules. At the University of Hawaii, biologist Clair Folsome has kept bacteria growing in sealed laboratory flasks since 1967. The colonies turn from green to red to purple but remain healthy despite the changing colors, which represent competition among oxygen and nonoxygen-producing forms. On the other end of the size spectrum, a group of people near Oracle, Arizona, are attempting to build Biosphere II—the largest artificial biosphere in existence. Like Biosphere I, Biosphere II is to be completely self-sustaining. And like the surface of the Earth—but unlike Folsome's test tubes and the ecospheres—it will include "biospherians": human beings (Fig. 30).

At completion, slated for 1990, Biosphere II promises to be the largest experimental biosphere in existence. Like some strange propagule of the Earth, it will cover about two and a half acres and will contain its own rivers and miniature ocean, complete with coral reefs. It will have marsh, desert, rain forest, and savannah habitats. Inside will be microbes, trees,

Figure 30.

shrubs, greenhouse crops, small food animals, and even a tool shop and a system of computers and electronic communication. Microbes to clean wastes from the soil, aphid-eating beetles to act as a natural pesticide, and many types of other ecologically sound organisms will be selected and included in the structure. With its special louvres or window slats designed to let in light at varying rates, an expandable "lung" that will allow it to adjust to changing atmospheric pressure, and communication links to scientists on the outside, Biosphere II will focus public attention on the need for harmony among people, technology, and nature.

Eight people, called "biospherians," have trained to live inside Biosphere II. They will be responsible for fertilizing plants, clearing grass, and performing other functions that in our biosphere are done by nonhuman organisms such as birds and large mammals. It will be hard. Everything inside will have to recycle. The air that the biospherians breathe will come from the green plants that are taking in carbon dioxide and giving off oxygen. The carbon dioxide exhaled by the biospherians will deliver carbon to the plants. When the plants breathe out carbon dioxide or when they die, the carbon dioxide given off in these processes will ultimately be consumed again by the biospherians. The biospherians will feed on the ancient freshwater fish *Tilapia,* grown in special tanks where the ammonia fish waste becomes nitrates that fertilize garden vegetables such as cucumbers and tomatoes growing directly in the water (Fig. 31). The closed ecology goes hand in hand with a frugal economy in which everything is used as completely as possible. If the biospherians waste their resources or contaminate their water or air, they will be in immediate trouble. It will not be possible for them, as it is for some in our Biosphere I, to escape their pollution, to "dump and run." It will become crystal clear in Biosphere II—as it is not yet to some

Figure 31.

in Biosphere I—that fouling our own nest is a losing game. The environment is a whole; "what goes round comes round." The eight biospherians will depend upon other organisms for their food, water, warmth, and their sense of life, fun, and well being.

One of the objectives of Biosphere II is to educate the rest of the world not just about Biosphere II but also about Biosphere I. Just as the space program's exploration of the lifeless desert of Mars and the poisonous clouds and scorching heat of Venus taught us to appreciate the beautiful blue Earth, so the establishment of a second complete living system containing humans will stress the sort of harmony we need in order to keep Biosphere I alive and well. While closed materially, Biosphere II will be open to light and in constant communication with Biosphere I. The biospherians will be connected by sight, telephone, television, radio, computer, and other electronic communications devices. Since they will not leave the structure—perhaps not for years—they need to keep in constant contact with scientific experts on the outside. From their efforts we stand to learn a lot about the ecological teamwork necessary to maintain closed systems with people in them. For example, as a result of various experiments to be performed in Biosphere II, scientists may be able to predict the probable outcome of environmental problems facing all of us. By covering the windows, the biospherians could mimic the "nuclear winter" of dust plumes and smoke predicted to spread and darken our whole atmosphere in the wake of a nuclear war. Although computer models have predicted freezing temperatures and the halting of plant growth, which would damage the entire living system, a three-dimensional model might be even more dramatic, detailed, and convincing. By manipulating Biosphere II's carbon dioxide levels, scientists could simulate the so-called greenhouse effect—a projected rise in temperature due to air pollution. Such demonstrations might have an impact on politicians and countries around the world. Biospheres therefore can be used as the tools to figure out the effects of global technology.

Another goal of Biosphere II is to serve as a prototype for life in space. Without such closed technology, there seems to be no way to live or travel for extended periods in outer space. Although half a million people are flying in airplanes and helicopters at any one time these days, no human has ever completed his life cycle in the atmosphere. For this cycle of birth, childhood, adolescence, maturation, mating, fertilization, and birth to occur totally in the air, much more time and coordination of nature and technology will be required.

Like the first successful airplane flights, we can expect the first journeys into man-made biospheres to be relatively short. But eventually the technology must be mastered. It is not just for people. It would be great insurance for life to be able to thrive off the planet. Also, biosphere technology being developed now might ultimately help life to outlast the sun. Astronomic theories suggest that billions of years from now the sun will expand to become a red giant, boiling away the Earth's oceans. Life has already existed for four billion years. Perhaps with biosphere technology it will ultimately be able to move to a new solar system and live much longer!

11

The Soviet Bios Project

Although political disharmony prevents us from getting really accurate information about certain scientific projects going on in the Soviet Union, we know that biospheric efforts have been under way there for some time. The Soviets have already announced their goal to settle Mars, and with a series of so-called "Bios" structures, they have been preparing for a manned mission there. Realistically, a round-trip voyage would take about three years. In preparation, two Soviet researchers were locked inside "Bios 3," a biospheric structure set up in Siberia. Although they took with them only one month's supply of food, the researchers reportedly stayed in Bios 3 for five months. The rest of their food, grown under xenon lamps, which have a light-output spectrum similar to the sun, was recycled, as were their air, water, and wastes.

Earlier Bios projects were as small as about 42.5 cubic feet (12 cubic meters), but twenty years of active Soviet research on closed ecosystem architecture has convinced them of the need to make larger, more complex structures. Bios 3 is about 11,120 cubic feet (315 cubic meters), almost the size of

Skylab, the orbiting space station put up by the United States in the seventies. Still, it is tiny.

By contrast Biosphere II will be over 35 million cubic feet (1 million cubic meters), much larger than anything of its kind (Fig.32). One reason scientists and engineers were reluctant at first to build large structures containing many species was that they seemed less predictable. Yet it appears now that the self-regulating, recycling properties of the biosphere can be more easily re-created in larger, more complex structures. Such size challenges the thinking of classical engineers, taught to methodically plan everything out in detail. The workings of the biosphere, however, are so complex that we will never understand them entirely. We must, at least to a certain extent, trust the natural tendencies of life to form stable, homeostatic systems. Nobody understands every aspect of a biosphere, yet we all live in one. So biospherians may have to add an artistic attitude to their scientific one: they already realize that living in new biospheres will entail depending not only on carefully worked out mechanical and electronic systems but also on self-adjusting machines—the far older, and ultimately more powerful technology of life itself.

Figure 32.

12

Living With Each Other and Nature

With the rise of biospherics and biosphere building, it seems only a matter of time before we see manned missions to Mars. And after that, who knows? Perhaps the Soviet and American nations, as well as others, will get together to settle Mars with life brought from biospheres. Right now, the surface of Mars is the harshest, most hostile desert we know (Fig. 33). It has less water, more ultraviolet radiation and colder temperatures than the worst Antarctic deserts. To survive outside on the surface of Mars, food and air will of course be needed. But can life adjust to such an alien environment? Can Mars perhaps be seeded with blue-greens and other hardy microbes that once upon a time turned the Earth from a rocky barren landscape into a fertile jungle brimming with life? Nations will need to work not only with other species and new technology, but also with each other to accomplish such a heroic task. Then perhaps the cosmos can be turned into a cosmic garden.

In a way, the view of nature inspired by the new science of biospherics and biosphere building brings us back to the

Figure 33.

ancients. Our ancestors believed the Earth—even the entire universe—to be alive. As we have seen, the Earth *is* like a giant organism in which we are only parts. We cannot expect to completely understand something of which we are only a fragment. But we can realize that other organisms are not solely means to be used for human ends. Each organism and group of organisms is an end in itself. To respect ourselves, we have to respect all of nature.

We contain in our bodies the biological ordering arising from interactions of many organisms working in dynamic harmony. This sort of coordination among many organisms leads to individuality arising at new, more inclusive levels. In a way the biosphere is becoming more individual, and yet, as it does so, it is sectioning off into new biospheres. Each of us is like the global self of which we are all a part. Small organisms grow, reproduce, and alter as they become parts of still larger organisms. The many levels of biology from cell to organism to biosphere begin to mirror one another.

As part of Biosphere I or inside Biosphere II, III, or IV all of us have to reevaluate our relationship to nature. Until very recently it made some sense to put ourselves above nature and assure ourselves that we could exploit everything around us without serious consequences. But we have come to realize that what is around us is part of us; human responsibility does not end at the surface of the skin, or with the family, church, ethnic group, or nation. A fundamental allegiance of each of us should be to the biological world as a whole—the Earth biosphere, which despite all our bloodletting and mischief has so far nurtured and sustained us. We do not live in a container but with other living, feeling beings. The Earth is alive. Inside or outside of experimental biospheres, all organisms are biospherians. We cannot conquer nature with our technology, but we can conquer our technological nature: by working with nature, by conceiving of life as a whole integrated organism of which we are part, we can use our ingenuity for the benefit of all life—and be the more human for it.

Glossary

abyss—The ocean depths below about 500 fathoms or 1000 meters.

aerobic—Needing oxygen. Organisms that need oxygen to live are called aerobic organisms.

anaerobic—Not needing oxygen. Organisms that must live in the absence of oxygen are called anaerobic organisms.

animal—A member of the Kingdom Animalia (see **five kingdoms**). Animals develop from hollow embryos that are formed by the union of an egg and a sperm.

atmosphere—The mixture of gases that surrounds a planet. On the Earth, the atmosphere is composed of almost 80 percent nitrogen and 20 percent oxygen, with small amounts of carbon dioxide, water vapor, hydrogen, methane, and other gases.

bacterium—A member of the Kingdom Prokaryotae (see **five kingdoms**). Bacteria do not have nuclei.

biosphere—The area at the surface of the Earth that contains everything necessary for life. The biosphere goes down about 6 miles (11 kilometers) into the abyss of the ocean and stretches up into the atmosphere about 4.6 miles (8 kilometers).

Biosphere I—Another name for planet Earth, the first biosphere known to humans.

biospherian—An organism that lives in a biosphere.

blue-green bacteria—Bacteria that are blue-green in color and release oxygen into the atmosphere during photosynthesis.

carrying capacity—The quantity of organisms an environment can support at any one time.

cell—The basic unit of living organisms. Cells are separated from their environment by a thin skin called a membrane. In some cases, one cell may itself be an *organism*.

chimaera—A creature from ancient Greek mythology that was made of the parts of many different kinds of animals.

community—A population of different types of organisms living in the same place at the same time.

deep-sea vents—Cracks in the ocean floor where heat and energetic chemicals escape from the inside of the Earth, creating an environment where some organisms can live.

ecospheres—Small closed aquariums containing organisms that survive by using solar energy and interacting with each other to recycle important elements and their own wastes.

ecosystem—A visible, separate unit in nature such as a pond or forest composed of communities of organisms. These organisms interact with each other and their local environment to cycle the elements important to life, such as carbon, sulfur, oxygen, hydrogen, nitrogen, and phosphorus.

embryo—An early stage in the development of many-celled organisms, produced from a fertilized egg.

encapsulation technology—Technology used to create enclosed environments such as submarines, space ships, and ecospheres.

evolution—Changes in organisms throughout the generations during the history of the Earth.

five kingdoms—Based on their cells and the way they live, all organisms on the Earth can be divided into five large groups called kingdoms. The five kingdoms are called Prokaryotae (the kingdom of bacteria), Protoctista (the kingdom of protoctists), Fungi (the kingdom of fungi), Plantae (the kingdom of plants), and Animalia (the kingdom of animals).

fungus—A member of the Kingdom Fungi (see **five kingdoms**). Fungi grow from spores. Molds and mushrooms are examples of fungi.

Gaia—The goddess of the Earth in ancient Greek mythology.

greenhouse effect—A rise in the overall temperature of the Earth because of the large amounts of heat-trapping greenhouse gases, like carbon dioxide, that are being put into the atmosphere. The industrial activities of humans, such as the burning of fossil fuels (oil, coal, gasoline), are largely responsible for the increase in these gases in recent history.

homeostasis—The process of making changes in parts of a system, usually as a reaction to an outside force, so that the system itself can stay the same.

mitochondria—Special structures inside cells that use oxygen to free the chemical energy of food so that it can be used by the organism to live and grow.

nuclear winter—A planetary chill predicted to follow a nuclear war. The season of cold would be caused by the dust and fragments from the huge explosions clouding the atmosphere and preventing solar energy from reaching the Earth.

nucleus—A structure surrounded by a membrane that contains most of the cell's genetic information.

organism—A living thing.

photosynthesis—The process that some organisms use to make food for themselves from sunlight and carbon dioxide.

pillow lavas—Pillow-shaped masses of hardened lava found on the ocean floor.

plant—A member of the Kingdom Plantae (see **five kingdoms**). Plants develop from embryos.

pollutant—Any substance an organism puts into its environment that is not re-used quickly and becomes harmful to life.

pollution—An excess of pollutants.

population—Individuals of the same type of organism living in the same place at the same time.

population controls—Anything, such as war, disease, and birth control, that limits the growth of a population.

propagules—Small structures made by organisms that can be moved from one place to another and that contain everything they need, given the right environmental conditions, to grow into a new organism. Spores and seeds are examples of propagules.

protein—Large molecule composed of long chains of carbon, hydrogen, oxygen, nitrogen, and sulfur. Proteins help to speed up chemical reactions in living organisms and are also important in their structure.

protoctist—A member of the Kingdom Protoctista (see **five kingdoms**). Protoctists are microorganisms with nuclei. Algae (including all seaweed) slime molds, and ciliates are examples of protoctists.

recycling—The process of re-using materials, such as the air, water, or the elements.

respiration—The breakdown of organic molecules (such as food) in order to get energy for the organism.

spaceship Earth—A name given to planet Earth because, like a spaceship, it travels in space. Modern spaceships, however, do not yet provide for their inhabitants as does the Earth, which recycles due to its natural biosphere.

spore—A small propagule of bacteria or fungi.

stratosphere—The region of the atmosphere above the troposphere that usually has horizontal winds, called the jet stream, and a stable temperature. On Earth, the stratosphere begins between 8 and 20 km, and extends to around 45 km above the planet's surface. The stratospheric temperature on Earth is about −75° C.

superorganism—A living thing, many of whose parts are also living things.

symbiosis—The living together by two or more organisms of different types that need each other to survive.

terraforming—Changing the surface of a planet so that it will become like Earth ("terra") and support life.

troposphere—The lowest layer of a planet's atmosphere that becomes colder as you go higher. On Earth, the troposphere begins at the planet surface and rises for about 10 to 20 km. This is where visible weather, such as cloud formation, occurs.

Further Reading

BOOKS

Allen, J., and Nelson, M. *Space Biospheres.* Oracle, Arizona: Synergetic Press, 1986.

Alvarez, L., et al. *Pioneering the Space Frontier:* The Report of the National Commission on Space. New York: Bantam Books, 1986.

Lovelock, J.E. *The Ages of Gaia.* New York: W.W. Norton, 1988.

Margulis, Lynn, and Sagan, Dorion. *The Microcosmos Coloring Book.* Cambridge, Massachusetts: Harcourt Brace Jovanovich, 1988.

Myers, N., editor. *Gaia, An Atlas of Planet Management.* Garden City, New York: Anchor Books, 1984.

Raymo, C. *Biography of a Planet.* Englewood Cliffs, New Jersey: Prentice Hall, 1984.

Vernadsky, V. *The Biosphere.* London: Synergetic Press, 1986.

PERIODICALS

Crichton, Wally. "Making Connections." *Science and Children,* February 1988, pp. 16–18.

Freundlich, N.J. "Biosphere." *Popular Science,* Vol. 229 (December 1986), pp. 54–56+.

McCourt, R. "Creating Miniature Worlds." *International Wildlife,* Vol. 18 (January/February 1988), pp. 38–40.

Maranto, G. "Earth's First Visitors to Mars." *Discover,* May 1987, pp. 28–43.

Robbins, Jim. "Visitors to a Small Planet: Earth, Meet Biosphere II." *The New York Times,* Sunday, October 18, 1987, Section 4, p. E–6.

Sagan, D. "Bioshelters." *Omni,* March 1987, pp. 54–59.

Weber, Bruce. "Noah's Ark: The Sequel." *The New York Times Magazine,* January 31, 1988, p. 62.

Index